A HANDBOOK

on

Being British

Alex Stranger-Onoh

Pen Press Publishers
London

© Alex Stranger-Onoh 2003

First published in 2002 by
Pen Press Publishers Ltd
39-41 North Road
London N7 9DP

ISBN 1-904018-45-9
Humour

A catalogue record of this book is available
from the British Library

Cover illustration by Mick Wright,
Concept by Alex Stranger-Onoh
Design by Jacqueline Abromeit

Dedication

This book is dedicated to my sister Lillian and my daughters Candy and Jija, who are my everything

Acknowledgements

Cynthia Ikhaluwa, God bless you always.
Julia Siddall, great typing, thanks.
Nana Florence Rides, the best Brit ever - more
healthy and happy years to you.

Finally, to all the Brits, who have provided me with
abundant material for my book, THANK YOU and
ever remain, TRUE BRITS.

Contents

INTRODUCTION

Being British! Being British does not merely entail living in Her Majesty's realm in brick houses or even castles that date back hundreds of years, just because you possess a valid British passport and diligently pay your taxes and National Insurance contributions. Neither does it end at casting your vote for the Tories, Labour and Liberal Democrats or any other raving party of your choice. Collecting your social benefits, pensions, council housing and enjoying, the heavily subsidised National Health Service will not conclusively seal you as a bona-fide Brit. Oh no!

Being British is far more complex, converse, complicated, convoluted, comic, compound, composite and yet, conservative, consistent, constitutional and, in fact, a complete conundrum.

At this point, I will request that you kindly pick your Oxford dictionary for reference, since part of being British, means being totally ignorant about the Queen's English in its perplexing entirety. But how can you tell if you are British enough? How can you be sure that you possess those typically British characteristics, beliefs, habits and behavioural patterns that categorically stamp you as a true citizen of this complex and unique race? And what exactly are these characteristics anyway? Well, carry on reading. Carry on? Ah, you've still got some grey matter up there, I see.

Well then let's get cracking!

THE WEATHER BUG

When not defeating Philip of Spain's Armada or frustrating Hitler's Blitz, the British weather devotes the rest of its time to keeping the citizens entertained, frustrated, exasperated and resigned but happy. Being British means being bitten by the British weather bug; in other words, having an obsessive and near fanatical interest in the whims and caprices of the weather, with sniffs and sneezes to ensure you remain focused. All your conversations must be pre-fixed, mid-fixed and end-fixed by lively references to the contradictory weather. Being British means that your favourite television program must be... guess? No, not Crossroads, Coronation Street? Come on get real! Emerdale? Eastenders? Blind Date? WRONG, WRONG, WRONG. Morons! The answer of course is the weather report! Yes, Michael Fish reigns supreme. While some races consult astrology and others consult soothsayers, or witch doctors or even the stock market in order to plan their daily activities, the Brits consult the weather report. This is

their number one fix, their Bible, their raison d'être.

So, being British means that you must adopt your crazy weather as your enemy and your salvation. Break the ice in uncomfortable and unfamiliar social or political situations with discussions on the unpredictable weather. Adjust your mood and fashion to suit the weather. Work your whole life round this demanding weather and when it gets too much to handle, escape to Ibiza, Marjorca, Tenerife, Minorca, the Costa del sol or the Caribbean Islands and spend the rest of your sunny holiday talking and wondering about that looney weather you abandoned at home to the tune of *"A foggy day in London town!"*

Congratulations! You are the real McCoy!

CULTURE PUB

Call it the pub, call it the local, it all boils down to one place, namely, the British favourite meeting and drinking place. Pub-crawling is the greatest national pastime. The British pub culture is an institution in itself. Going back hundreds of years, this is one tradition that has survived the test of time. Located at every creek and corner of the realm, pubs are the hub of the British social scene. These pubs pride themselves in flaunting far-out names such as THE KING'S HEAD, THE MARKER'S ARMS, THE THREE BANDITS, PIG IN A HOLE. etc. etc.

The less imaginative ones usually content themselves with adopting the names of the streets or areas they are located in. Thus, a pub in the Coundon area will be called, "The Coundon" while one in Holyhead Road would be called "The Holyhead". Very imaginative, wouldn't you say?

Anyway, pub-crawling gives the Brits the opportunity to socialise in an informal and relaxed environment, watch sports events on live multi-screens, drink pints and gallons of lager, enjoy hot and cold meals, listen to good music, play darts, snooker or what other games are on offer and generally unwind after a hectic day at the office, at home or at the Benefits Office. Pubs vary of course and have different environments and atmosphere. But a pub is a pub, is a pub to the true Brit. Being British means enjoying your under-measure pints and if dissatisfied, organising a "campaign for Real Ale" to ensure your government introduces laws to force your publican to pull a full pint of beer in case you've been getting short-changed. That way, you can drown in your full measure pints till you become a veritable yob and provide "yobologist" professor Dick Hobbs ample material to study and report. If nothing else, at least you'll get nicely re-classed as a "M.V.V.D" (male vertical volume drinker), while getting arrested for pissing pure alcohol on Nelson's Column in Trafalgar Square.

So unless you are in the geriatric age bracket and prefer your daily bingo to your local pub, why don't you confirm your Britishness by finding your way to your nearest pub and offering a "here's to you, gaffer!" to your friendly and accommodating Guvnor. Already there? Ah, well, congratulations then to another true Brit.

FOOTBALL CRAZY

Football or Cricket. One or the other or both. Yes, you've got it in a nutshell; Being British means being either a football fanatic or a cricket enthusiast or, possibly, both. The blue bloods and country Brits usually favour the horsey sports like polo, horse riding and the controversial fox-hunting. Rugby is another possible contender. However, the vast majority of he British population live, drink and breathe football! The British football hooligans are known and dreaded world-wide because of their rather unbridled enthusiasm for their clubs. Good club managers are revered, while incompetent ones are reviled. This is one game that has no half-measures. It's all or nothing!

Being British means being prepared to sacrifice your time, your money, your marriage and, occasionally, your life for your club. Cricket, being the "gentleman's sport", attracts rather fewer rowdy fans but support is very high nonetheless and Ian Botham lives eternally in our memories. But football is the true national craze. Strikers,

defenders, midfielders, goal keepers and all other positions in the game, are all kings and heroes to their loyal fans. So, Rio, Beckam, Owen, Seaman and Keane are house-hold names in football - crazy Britain. Let the memory of the recently concluded 2002 World Cup celebrations in the realm be a reminder of what football means to this nation. Mega - screens were set up in schoos for children to watch Goran Erikson's

England team in action BEORE the start of their Lessons! Church services were re-scheuled to accomodate the equally football - crazy congregation and if you were unfortunate enough to have your wedding scheduled for the day England played Argentina, then chances are that neither your groom nor the registrar would have turned up to do you the honours. It was even rumoured that the Queen's favourite Corgies were not taken out for their walk on that memorable day because, Her very glorious magesty, Queen Elizabeth herself, was actually glued to the T. V set, watching her boys repeat the Falkland experience on a thoroughly humiliated Argentina, in stupendous history-making football! So, now you know it; from the highest and mightiest to the lowest, humblest and yougest in the realm, football is simply, pure nectar! If you do not already have a favourite club you support, nor queue up to get club paraphernalia autographed under rain, frost, snow or sleet, then you are definitely not being British enough. Spurs, Liverpool, Newcastle, Manchester United, Sheffield, Chelsea, Coventry, Leeds etc, etc, just find yourself a home club and a premiere club to support and revere. Then, and only then, can you rightly claim to Being truly British.

LET'S GET CRITICAL

Being British means being a born critic. Your average British man, woman and child is a professional critic! However, the unique aspect about the British form of criticism is that it is inwardly turned. By this, I mean that the British just love to criticise their government and their country. Their press is on a rollercoaster ride to perennial orgies of criticism - the prize or price of a world-acclaimed democracy. Perhaps, they might need a dose of a banana republic to appreciate what they've got. But then, it is doubtful if a stint in a germ-riddled, bug-infested goal would do the trick. They are British, you see, and the Brits must criticise for their sanity and the sheer bloody–mindedness of it.

Being British means being prepared to criticise the National Health Service, the education system, the transport system, the Social Service, the exorbitant taxes, the Government's policies and even the state of your neighbour's garden. Regardless of the fact that Britain has got one of the strongest currencies in the world, that

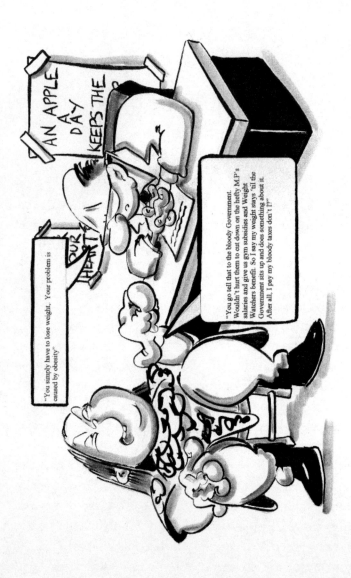

the British standard of education is considered among the highest, if not the highest in the globe, that Britain is privy to one of the strongest democracies in the world and enjoys unlimited religious, political, social and economic freedoms, our true Brit would nonetheeless find something, no matter how insignificant, to criticise about the realm.

Then, on one cold and wet winter's day, after happily criticising the dreadful weather, your true Brit would relax in front of his high tech TV set, inside his council or mortgaged house obtained through positive government policies and watch CNN flash news after news of world disasters and tragedies. Then, and only then, would he shake his head in sympathy, phone up to make a generous donation (don't forget the Brits just love to donate to all causes imaginable) then thank God that Britain has been spared the terrible earthquake, volcano, famine, hurricane, civil war, religious repression, military dictatorship, torture or currency devaluation.

Still, he'll muse, the British government ought to be doing more to improve the plight of those poor bulls in Spain! What can I say? Yes, it is indeed a fact of life. Your true Brit is a critical chap and if you find you simply have to criticise my criticisms, then congratulations, you are only being true to yourself – a bona fide Brit.

CARRY ON LAUGHING

Being British means being an undiscovered comic. This race has one of the wackiest sense of humour in the universe. The fascinating thing about British humour is that, like the Brits themselves, it is very subtle, dry and tongue-in-cheek, unlike, say, the sledge-hammer brand of American humour. The true Brit will wryly laugh at himself and gleefully laugh at you. You just can't win with this chap. His language is inundated with words and expressions that could have numerous inter-pretations and your true Brit knows how to exploit these double meanings for maximum humorous effect. If you are a foreigner and are not sure of what British humour is all about, just grab yourself a copy of the riotous "Carry On's" or "Dad's Army" or better still, "Jeeves and Wooster" films to get a good idea of British hu-mour at its best - or worst, depending on which end of the spectrum you find yourself.

On the literary side, a couple of Tom Sharpe novels would give you a full dose of the British brand of wicked humour and malapropisms. I promise you'll emerge from this brilliant experience most enlightened, and emotionally lightened, by the stress-busting good laughs you would have enjoyed. The British humour you see, is so witty and satirical, that a stranger, unused to the quirks and puns in the language, may have to listen over and over again, in the hope of cottoning on to the jokes. Ask some poor Americans that have been interviewed by Frank Skinner and you get a general idea of what I mean. British humour is totally spontaneous and striking in its subtlety and wit. Take this classic example;

A flick of Mariah Carey on national television, dancing to her latest hit, dressed in nothing more than a pair of skimpy micro-shorts and an equally flimsy top. Then, the voice of the reporter announcing Virgin's twenty million pound pay-off to terminate Mariah's contract. The reporter concludes by hoping that Mariah will find a safe pocket to keep her eight figure payoff in.

"Not in those shorts!" quips the newscaster poker-faced, before coolly going to the next item of news! Vintage British humour! Absolutely priceless! Other people might spend time wondering about the eight-figure sum, the circumstances of the pay-off or the morality of the pay-off. But not the true Brit. He will first take the mickey out of the issue before going on to more mundane matters without as much as a "by your leave". This is a race to whom nothing and no-one is sacrosant. They would take the mickey out of God and the Queen without a blink of the eye. The wickedly hilarious Spitting Image series will give you a pretty good idea of this race's peculiar brand of humour.

The British humour is so in-born that even the most dour of individuals will frequently crack the odd dry joke and keep a straight face while everyone else is doubled up in laughter. This is a race that thrives on its ability to laugh at itself, be that self, the halitosis or ginger pubes. So now you know it - being British means possessing this unique priceless gift of a wicked, subtle and utterly riotous wit as a matter of course. That said, have you then got what it takes to be British with regard to humour? Yes?

Then carry on laughing!

BRIGHTEST AND BEST AREN'T THE SONS OF THE EMPIRE

Being British means being the master of the understated. In emotions and speech, in romance and love, in houses and cars, clothes and fashion, you name it, the Brit believes in playing things down. So with regard to your style and colour of clothes, kindly ensure you are being British by choosing dull drab styles and very muted colours. This is because to the true Brit, loud is crass and bright is coarse. Greys, blues, browns and tans are in. Reds, yellows, oranges and tropical colours are definitely out, except perhaps when on holiday abroad. Take as many pictures as you like in these ghastly un-British colours while abroad. Just kindly ensure that they are safely stored away before you set foot back in the in the realm. Otherwise you may find yourself liable for a number of involuntary coronary attacks – just joking! But still a word of caution; please remember you are British when shopping for your clothes. Not for you the Hollywood colour scheme. "I'm gonna match my car" with my dresscode. Oh no! Instead, as a true Brit, you have to match your clothing to your British weather, which amounts to one thing; dull, dull, and dull. And, please, don't say, "Princess Diana (rest her soul) got away with it." She was a Princess and roaming royal ambassador. Do I hear you mutter "Joan Collins? Naomi Campbell?" Do you consider yourself in their league? Listen mate, unless you are a star or rather, a superstar, then stay off the glamour and be a Frost, a Kilroy-Silk, a Cilla, an Esther or a Robinson if you must dress like stars. Those are true Brits for you.

Go easy on furs. Remember that this is a race that loves animals. Finally, leave the gems and stones to the Royals and those classless American tourists. Plain and simple British gold from H-Samuel or Avon is as high as you can go without incurring the contempt, disdain and amused criticisms of your neighbours. This is one country where brightest isn't necessarily the best.

So, tell me, are you now being Britishly dull? Or un-Britishly bright?

"I WANT TO BE ALONE"

Need I say more? The heading speaks for itself. The Brits are an intensely private race. They value their privacy greatly and guard it jealously. This is because the Brits are terribly suspicious as a race. They distrust anything new, unfamiliar or non-conforming. This is a conservative race, taciturn by nature and very self-reliant. Don't forget that this is the race that popularised D.I.Y. Every true Brit has an understanding of D.I.Y, no doubt to prevent an invasion of their precious private sanctuaries by unknown, outside work persons; albeit, they may claim the reduced expense as the reason for their D.I.Y addiction. But now you know better.

Not for the Brits is the open exchange of confidences practiced freely by other nations. Not for them is the popular usage of shrinks as witnessed in the United States. Neither is the "bare-it-all" television exposures of private domestic affairs popular, dispite attempts to enforce the "compliance by constancy" policy adopted by some television studios. But it doesn't matter how many times he watches such exposés on TV, your true Brit would rather keep his thoughts and problems to himself. He will respect your privacy as long as you respect his, though he's free to criticise your life-style or whatever else takes his fancy, behind your back, without jeopardising your right to privacy and his right to free-speech and opinions.

Don't butt in unannounced, don't invade his space uninvited, don't be too familiar even when friendship has been established and please, please, however long your acquaintance, do not ask embarrassingly intimate questions. The rule here is "give as much as you receive and take as much as is accepted, step matching step, miles on par".

So now you know what being privately British means. Keep the following poem to heart, you can't go wrong with it.

SHUT YOUR TRAP
UNLESS YOU'RE PISSED
THEN ALL HAIL
THE LAGER – LOUT
SOD BLARNEY STONE
BARE YOUR SODDEN ARSE
OTHERWISE, IT'S
STIFF, UPPER LIP'S
'CAUSE
MUM'S THE WORD.

MY FAIR LADY... AND GENT

The British sense of fair play is legendary. The popular expression "good sportsmanship" must have been coined specifically with this race in mind. For, being British means, placing integrity and fairness high on your list of virtues. A Brit will work relentlessly to ensure that even his worst enemy is treated fairly, even if not scrupulously. If you are legally inclined, check out the rules governing the objective tests of liability in civil cases and the subjective test of culpability applied in criminal cases. Then you will understand the major role fairness plays in the intricate judicial processes and doctrines developed over centuries of trial and error. It's all EQUITY, EQUITY, EQUITY!

Britain has become the bane of most repressive governments and dictatorships world-wide and takes great pride in appearing meticulously fair in her domestic and foreign affairs. What other country would worry about the fair treatment of highly dangerous, convicted criminals or treacherous, unpatriotic citizens in foreign gaols and, go further by pledging huge sums to rebuild enemy territory destroyed in the course of action? Being British, therefore means offering to make tea for your colleagues in the office when you feel like getting yourself a nice hot drink, because it's only fair to do so. It means offering to meet your parents, siblings, friends, lovers and colleagues half-way with regard to bills, car, house-share and work-loads, because it's the only fair thing to do. It is also only fair to treat your youngsters as equals even if they are running wild with the excess liberty fairly given. It is also fair, not to break appointments without prior notification and not to keep one waiting at a rendezvous. It is equally fair to wait your turn at queues and beg peoples's pardon or murmur "sorry" a thousand times a day in case you have unconsciously breached some rules of fairness.

So, in a nutshell, being British means adopting the Rotary International creed to its fullest by asking yourself at all times in your thoughts, words and action,

"Is it the truth?
Is it fair to all concerned?
Will it build goodwill?
And better friendships?
Is it beneficial to all concerned?"

If you are not already consciously or unconsciously practising these ethics, then you are not being a fair lady or gent.

Did I hear someone, perhaps an ex-colonial, mention scruples? Stolen artifacts still remaining at the British Museum perhaps? Ahh, but scruples are another matter altogether with the Brits – we are merely talking fairness here and I shall constrain myself to that until another day. It simply wouldn't be fair to mix up issues here, would it now? It just wouldn't be British.

Alex Stranger-Onoh

SAY IT WITH FLOWERS

Being British means to scrupulously remember and celebrate anniversaries. From births to deaths, engagements, weddings to divorces, Christmas, new-year and Easter, the Queen's Jubilee, Rememberance Day other wise known as poppy day, christenings - everything that can possibly be celebrated or remembered is given high priority by the Brits. For what the Brits lack in expressiveness, they compensate adequately with anniversary gifts and celebrations. It is interesting to note that the quality or quantity of gifts given, does not necessarily reflect or correspond to the level of affection, friendship, dislike or indifference felt. Yes, it is a known fact that the Brits even give anniversary gifts or at least a card to people they may not particularly like or know well. But then, it is only the FAIR thing to do, isn't it? Being British and all.

So in case you are unfamiliar with this strange race, remember that being British means never forgetting to celebrate any type of anniversary and to graciously express appreciation for gifts received. Even the Royal Family are not oblivious to this tradition. The Queen personally sends a telegram to anyone who makes it to 100 years of age. And if you are not sure what would be suitable to give, why not just say it with flowers? Because being British means loving flowers, plants and a nice flower garden. It doesn't matter if your garden is at the rear, side or front of your house, or if the garden is large, medium or small. Arbour, conservatory, greenhouse or aviary: Fountains, arches, gnomes and rabbits: Garden shed, fancy pots or crazy paving - whatever takes your fancy, do it to that little, or if you're lucky, large patch of tended land that is an absolute must for the sanity and serenity of the truly British.

So now you know - being greenly British, means having and loving your garden to bits and enjoying your roses and posies as the seasons change. So, are you still being British? Have you given somebody a bunch of fresh flowers recently? If yes, you're in, if not you're out.

So sod-off you impostor, till you reform!

WHAT'S LOVE GOT TO DO WITH IT

Listen carefully; this is the story of the great debate on the British male and romance. The question is, "Is it hot, or is it cold? Do the French, Italians, Americans and the rest of the world truly have the edge over the Brits in that department or not?" Well then, let's examine what British romance is all about to the British man. If you are looking to hook up with this chap, the first thing to realise is that

i-   He will definitely not pinch your bottom in public

ii-   He will not sing you a serenade beneath your bay or double- glazed windows

iii-   He will not blow you extravagant kisses with weedy arms out- stretched dramatically

iv-   He will not grab a bunch of flowers without paying and chase you down a crowded street to offer it to you on bended knees

v-   He will not shout "I love you, cara mia" while

wining and dining you in a busy restaurant

vi- He will not buy you a car, rent you a flat nor single-handedly foot all your bills, especially your eating out and utility bills – it just wouldn't be fair, would it? Things should be 50-50 including love

vii- He will not buy you a diamond studded cartier watch unless you are as rich as Posh Spice and can give him a golden or better, platinum ball in return

viii- He will not take you on an all-expenses paid cruise around the world nor deck you out in haute couture, unless, perhaps, you are Naomi and can afford yours anyway

ix- He will certainly not give you carte blanche access to his credit cards however often you call him "honey, sweetie-pie or cutie-pants". Incidentally, this very reserved chap would cringe at these terms of endearment - so take things easy and think of other devious ways to relieve him of his hard-earned cash.

x- Finally, this honourable chap will not invite you to a menage-à-trois with his mistress or marry three extra wives to give you the dubious honour of belonging to the first wives club. You'll be numero uno or nothing!

Having said all this, what then can you expect from your seemingly dull British valentino-wanna-be? Well, the main thing to expect from this romantic sceptic is sincerity, devotion and in most cases, fidelity, while it lasts! While it lasts, you ask? But of course. The generation that celebrated silver and golden jubilees are long gone, consigned to the dustbin of pre-internet romance. These days you take what you get and keep what you take for as long as you can.

Your average Brit, as you may have noticed, has a desperate need to pair up. This desperation to team up is worse in the British female than in the male. This is because the British man has his mates, his football and his pub to keep him well-centred. For this reason, pairing up romantically does not have a priority rating in his life's agenda. The British female, on the other hand, may only have her job and family to provide her with distraction. For this reason, she may get so desperate to find a 'mate' which she won't find in her male compatriots, that in frustration, she may decide to go further afield to foreign shores to find romance - hence the rather racy reputation they seem to have acquired abroad over the years.

Anyhow, this desperation to pair up can at times result in some rather unsuitable, incompatible and even bizarre partnerships, a sure recipe for romantic crash-landings even before take-off. However, when the pairing is right and all the basic ingredients for a fine romance are there, then you can be in for some rather startling revelations. As mentioned earlier, the British are masters of subtlety in everything, including romance.

Your British man is just too realistic and down-to-earth for frills and moreover, the true Brit believes in the adage "Look, look and look yet again before leaping into anything" be the leaping into EU, the Euro or romance. Consequently, he will take his time to declare himself and commit to any relationship. He will play his cards close to his chest and check all pros and cons before jumping in. Fortunately, he is one lucky bastard because he is blessed with a long-suffering and patient breed of womankind. The British woman stands by her man through thick, and drink, through major and petty crime and through prostitute-mingling. She is that quintessential faithful dog who throws in the towel and leaves an abusive home, only, when death stares her in the face. She will patiently endure his vacillations, as he tries to decide between her, his freedom and his mates. She thinks nothing of having his kids out of wedlock if he so desires. She is your typical homing pigeon, accommodating, loving and generally unconfrontational.

Still, when eventually your British man finally does pitch his tent with you, you can expect the following:

i-   100% devotion

ii- 90% love. The remaining 10% is reserved for his mates, football, the pub and his hobbies

iii- 60% romance - expect flowers, chocolates and kitchen utensils or weighing scales

iv- 100% good, honest, caring and sizzling sex once the lights are dimmed, the sheets are cotton and you tell him his pecker is perfect.

Finally, a word of caution. Expect to perpetually be at war with his daily newspaper and weekend sports television. Your true Brit loves his daily paper for crosswords, racing results, football scores and cricket updates. Respect these boundaries, his mates and his pub-crawling and you will find yourself in for a fine romance as he loves you tenderly and will never let go of you.

TO BE ...OR NOT TO BE

The British respect and admire talent, hardwork, achievement and knowledge gained from experience, while other nations and races might place heavy emphasis on academic qualifications obtained from higher institutions. Sheer grit in whatever line of work you are engaged in, is all that is required. You are dealing with a race that rewards achievers with national honours, regardless of their academic qualifications or lack of them. Names like Sir Richard Branson and ex-Prime Minister John Major come to mind. These are self-made men who have pulled themselves through the ranks to reach the highest posts in their respective fields, through sheer hard work, talent and determination. For this reason, they have been duly recognised by their countrymen and Queen and widely acclaimed worldwide.

To the true Brit time is precious and punctuality vital. Forget the French and their siesta; The British plan their work and then work their plan as the saying goes. You must prove your worth and earn your pay. So do not assume that an armful of paper qualifications and degrees will automatically give you a definite edge in the work place over experienced employees that have put in years of loyalty and hard-work, gaining valuable knowledge in the process but without degrees. They will probably get an OBE or a peerage before you and your Degrees have done the rounds of futile interviews and been turned down for being over qualified without the necessary experience.

This is a nation where the teenagers are already gainfully employed at a pretty early age, either in delivering papers, in telesales or as part-time shop assistants. They start storing up knowledge in their teens, that can amount to a daunting wall of experience by the time the graduate is ready to attend his first interview. Despite efforts by successive governments to place more and more emphasis on the acquisition of degrees, as is the case in the United States and Germany, your average British person would rather start at an early age to earn his keep in an attempt to achieve total independence as swiftly as possible. He does not want to be beholden to any man, animal or king, thank you. The sooner he becomes king of his own mortgaged castle, the happier he will be. He is amply assisted in this laudable goal by employers who insist on rewarding excellence rather than admiring paper certificates without experience. These employers merely reflect the belief of this unique race, that at the end of the day, a man is valued for what he is than for what he has.

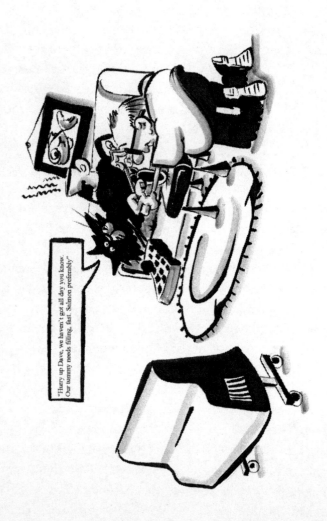

CATS AND DOGS

While other races boast or moan about their extended families, being British means recognising only one extended family member, namely, your household pet. This is one relation that needs no invitations to visit nor gets any restrictions on arrival. He is petted, feted, spoilt and indulged. There are no limits to the level of intimacy he can achieve with the rest of the family. Grown men and women play the fool with him while children play games with him. Practically every house has a household pet. Dogs, cats, mice, bunnies, snakes, tortoises and budgies are among the preferred type of extended family members though some may go for the exotic, as in monkeys, if they wish. But, the undisputed king, is the faithful dog, closely followed by the independent and some might say, selfish cat.

A visit to the local vet's will validate this assertion. Cats and dogs abound but the canine population inevitably supersedes that of the feline one. Thus, one can safely say that the Brits are a race of dog-lovers. Mary had a little lamb in the countryside of course but examine closely and you'll find that she also had a faithfull Sheepdog, Bulldog and Great Dane in residence. Faithful, you ask? But of course, faithful. And why not, I ask you, when they get fed gourmet meals and fancy snacks, receive special grooming and workouts. They have cute names and fancy collars and better still, get to visit the vet, the friends and even join the hunt while that social-climbing cat is out visiting the Queen. I tell you, I honestly don't understand why such derogatory expressions like "gone to the dogs", "dog eared" or "it's a dog's life", have not been removed from the dictionary. Because, believe me, these British dogs have never had it so good. Check out the luxurious coats of Her Majesty Queen Elizabeth II's pampered Royal dogs and tell me that they have "a dog's life".

Cats, morover, perpetually look as if they have "had the cream". British cats get the creamiest life of luxury with their owners, which explains why they aspired to play the fiddle and visit the Queen in London. Special catflaps are built for them for easy access in and out of the house while they live their nocturnal lives. Cosy cat baskets are abandoned for expensive leather couches by the fire-side while they lazily sleep their days away in preparation for their clandestine nightly activities, benignly smiled upon by their owners. I tell you, British pets on the whole, are in perpetual pets' paradise. This explains why poor old Mother Hubbard not only had a dog that read newspapers while she was out running errands for it, but why she ended up, poor thing, being the servant of the spoilt dog. Believe me British nursery rhymes do truly reflect the reality of the position of pets in your average British home - little queens and dictators.

This is a race that love their pets. Your true Brit will place his pet above himself in everything. He will fervently support the efforts of The R.S.P.C.A and do his bit to assist in the rescue efforts of animal victims of cruelty at home and abroad. So, if your house hasn't already been turned upside down, and furniture, shoes, carpets, and books destroyed by a puppy or kitten as they are trained into adult tyrants, then I'm sorry to tell you now that you are not being British.

ARE YOU BEING SERVED?

Ignore the myth of "fish and chips" for the hoi polloi and "roast and steak" for the other classes. Once upon a time, the British used to savour their traditional cuisine and took great pride in the good old British Breakfast of bacon, sausages, eggs, mushrooms, toast, muffins, porridge oats, juice and tea. I'm starving just writing about this. I bet you are too. These days though, things have radically changed in the meals department but, thankfully, the great old British Breakfast has so far survived the blitz.

For a race so proud and protective of its heritage, the British have happily absorbed the foreign and exotic into their diet. Being British, with the possible exception of those living in the country, means eating everything but British dishes. INDIAN curry, ITALIAN pizzas and cappuccinos, CHINESE take-aways, AMERICAN Kentucky fried chicken and fries, GERMAN frankfuters, DUTCH cheese, FRENCH croissants and wine bought on a day's trip to Calais, "swiss-rolls" etc,

etc, etc. Yes, yes I guess I'm taking things a bit too far. But seriously, a look around the cities in Britain will show you a place littered with restaurants and take-away outlets of every foreign cuisine you can imagine. The good old fish and chip shops are fast becoming a thing of the past, but for the efforts and patronage of faithful football fans. Even fruit and vegetables and a whole range of products sold in supermarkets are from counties other than Britain, like apples from France and beet from Belgium. About 70% of organic food found in Britain is foreign. Things have gotten so bad that the government have started looking for ways to reconnect home-grown food and the British public as a whole, as well as encouraging supermakets to do their bit in promoting British food. Whether or not they will succeed is another matter altogether. You can take a horse to the water but you cannot force it to drink, as the saying goes. Your average Brit's taste buds have been so radically altered by years of "Turkish and Asian delights" that, it remains to be seen how successful the "Grown in England" campaign will be in bringing about a change.

Still, it's not such a terrible thing, this food globalisation trend. So, are you being served? If yes, Bon Appetit!

"ALL THINGS DRAB AND BEAUTIFUL"

Kindly pay attention! What I'm about to tell you is a vital and intrinsic component to this conundrum called The British. Being British with the possible exception of the townies, means that you must remember the past, honour the past and treasure the memory of the past kept alive by daily audio-visual reminders throughout the realm. The theme is: Antiques! Antiques! Antiques! The older, drabber and to some people, uglier, the better and more highly valued and treasured.

Be it Roman, Norman, Tudor, Stuart, Elizabethan or Victorian, treasure the great relics of the past. Nothing is junk unless it's new. New belongs to the Hollywood set. New is crass. New is classless. New is totally un-British. You must remember we're dealing with a race that is surrounded by its past. A people that live in houses centuries-old in an age of space-travel and see no reason for modernising "It's a listed building, you see, so no double-glazing, thank you". Every home must have its family heirloom, no matter how small; Items handed down from generation to generation, treasured and revered, filled with rich history and adventure, worthy of the great name, antique!

So, if you are planning on dwelling in the realm of the Brits or consider yourself a bona fide Brit, then do remember that being British means placing great value on all your old paraphernalia, your old buildings, vintage cars and even your old customs, traditions, habits and conventions - we must not forget to set the clock forward and backward. Why? Because nobody else does it, that's why. Incidentally, remember to keep left if you are a driver. So what if the rest of the world drives right - they're on the wrong side of the road. So kindly keep left and hurry up before one misses the changing of the guards.

So, in conclusion, being British means adopting the British creed in these matters;

"Out with the new
In with the old,
God save the Queen."

HEAD AND SHOULDERS

When it comes to the area of personal grooming, your average British code is simple enough to follow, mainly stick to Head and Shoulders as much as you can. This is because, being British means remembering to value your hair more than the rest of your body and your teeth. Manufacturers and retailers have cottoned on to the British hair craze and are making a killing in sales of hair products. We all know about the popular British advice about giving your hair 100 strokes of the brush every night. It is for real; perhaps not exactly at night but count the number of strokes your average British hair receives in any given day, and it will amount to one hundred or more. This race loves colour on their hair (check out the punks for extreme colours) and loves getting a regular cut, hence the proliferation of barber shops in the realm.

Once your average Brit gets past his head, it's doubt-ful if the rest of his body beneath the shoulders will receive favourable treatment. The British teeth has long

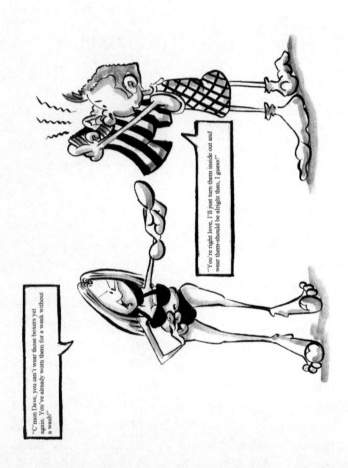

been the victim of grooming neglect, although an increased awareness, thanks to the efforts of the health and romance industries, has brought some welcome changes. Despite all that, being British means to never, ever floss! That's too American. Flash your brown teeth and braces proudly and scorn your dentist till you need new dentures. Never, ever cap or polish. This would give you unbritishly white and even teeth. As regards your nails, either bite the nails painfully down to the skin or neurotically manicure ten times a day.

Be best friends with your deodorant and have a bath only when it's absolutely necessary. If you're a bloke and things get too bad, turn your boxers inside out and be pretty liberal with the aftershave. Don't forget to dab methylated spirits on the various pierced parts of your face and anatomy and regularly re-purchase new earrings and studs to replace the ones damaged by the methylated spirit.

Smelly socks and Athlete's Foot are no strangers to your true Brit and Dhobie Itch and the occasional lice can sometimes cramp his lackadaisical grooming style. And, finally, in matters of physical fitness, Being British means to shun the gym and sod the jog. Those are too desperately American. Instead be proud if your British pear-shape and pub-induced pot-belly and if things get too bad, simply get Reductil from your G.P on the National Health and hope that one day, this terrible government will see the sense in offering you the slimming pill absolutely free of charge.

After all, it's only fair that the government should pay for your obesity if it expects to get the best out of you at the work place.

So now you know what being British means in personal grooming, a mixed-grill of filth and mint.

GOD SAVE THE QUEEN

As the French guillotined their aristocrats, the Russians bayoneted theirs and the vast majority of the world either exciled theirs or democratically voted them out of existence, the contradictory Brits elevated their royals to the divine, changed their minds and executed them, then reinstated them again to the tune of "God save the King/Queen".

The Brits are a race that value their past and fiercely guards its preservation. The institution of the monarchy is so entrenched in British history that it may well take a overwhelming majority of radical labour votes (if that) to put an end to this time-honoured symbol of continuity. And don't forget that this is a race of very conservative people, who will resist drastic changes, even while at times voting in change-touting Labour in their contrariness and determination to uphold their treasured freedom of choice. The British attachment and determination to preserve the Royal institution is clearly evident in the lyrics of the National Anthem

Alex Stranger-Onoh

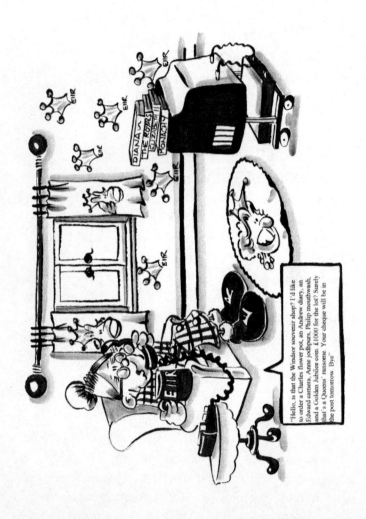

God save our gracious Queen,
Long live our noble Queen,
God save our Queen,
Send her victorious,
Happy and glorious,
Long to reign over us:
God save our Queen.

Thy choicest gifts in store
On her be pleased to pour,
Long may she reign.
May she defend our laws,
And ever give us cause
To sing with heart and voice,
God save our Queen.

Now I ask you, does any of this sound like a people that are ready in any foreseeable future to do away with their Royal Family? Charles, Ann and Andrew may divorce and/or re-marry - that's neither here nor there. After all, King Henry VIII, the founder of the Church of England, married six wives. So, the anti-Royalists that hold unto the modern divorces (among other grievances) as an excuse to vote out the monarchy, know where to go with their whinging - back to where they can remain kings in their own castles while the rest of the nation bask in the security and joy of knowing that yet another long-lasting institution of the realm is still thankfully, preserved. The magnificent celebration of the Queen's Golden Jubilee by the nation is a testament to the enduring love and loyalty The British bear for their monarchy. Our anti-Royalist should also remember that they are dealing with a main tourist attraction and the continual influx of foreign currency, to brighten up the day of the Chancellor of the Exchequer.

So, if you consider yourself truly British, you must have a lively interest in the affairs and "affairs" of the Royal Family. You either love the Royal Family, hate the Royal Family or criticise the Royal Family. But, one thing you can never do is to ignore the Royal Family because they are too firmly entrenched in all facets of your daily life to be ever completely ignored or forgotten. From your pounds to your stamps, the image of the Queen remains ever fresh in your consciousness as a Brit. Even the press get vital and exciting materials from the affairs of the Royal Family to keep the nation constantly interested.

So remember, being truly British entails having a healthy or even unhealthy interest in the ever fascinating institution of the British monarchy as tourists continue to pour into the realm to watch the gates of Buckingham Palace in the hope of catching a glimpse of HER MAJESTY

RAIDERS OF THE LAST VALUE-PACK

Being British means being a professional bargain hunter. This race could possibly be the thriftiest race in the whole world. The Brits believe in getting value for their money - a thousand times over! Voucher hunting is a lively national pastime with this race. Even a one pence voucher, cut out of a magazine or tabloid, will be jealously guarded like a treasure hoard. Shops and supermarkets had better be prepared to make it worth your while to shop with them if they want to get a piece of your Sterling cake. From Sainsbury's reward cards to Boots cards, you name it, you'll find the ubiquitous offer. The big names in the high streets have fast learned that this unique race insists on getting more than their rightful share of bargains from them. So they offer rewards and incentives from petrol vouchers to holiday vouchers, cash discounts to free offers, all in a desperate bid to please these bargain fanatics called the British!

Airlines and travel agents have learned that bargain

"I'm certainly not going to pay you full fare when everyone else is giving an Xmas discount. I'd rather walk home than line your stingy pockets"

fares and holidays are the fastest way to get the patronage of our thrifty Brit. As one slighted air-passenger
said righteously, that if British Airways weren't prepared
to offer good fare incentives, then he will not offer them
his patronage either. Rather, he would fly "Go" Airlines that do offer more attractive bargains. It is not
therefore surprising to find sales going on almost all
year round in this realm. These sales offer the Brits the
opportunity to bargain hunt to their heart's content. The
retail industry has learnt how to pander to the Brits'
bargain mania without jeorpadizing their own profits.
They have discovered the 99p trick! So, while your thrifty
Brit is busy thinking he has got himself a cracking bargain at the decent price of four quid and a bit, he actually ends up paying nearer five pounds because the £4.99
label has worked its deceptive trick on this bargain
sucker. At the end, a whole one pound extra has subtlely
been extracted from him with a one pence change gravely
returned to ensure that he is constantly kept in a happy
state of thinking that he has scored one over the big
shot retailers.

Your thrifty Brit is prepared to change his electric,
gas or telephone supplier as many times as it takes to
find the cheapest rates, even by a few pennies. But a
word of caution; Do not confuse this race's bargain
compulsion for quality reduction. One will soon find
that near-expired goods prominently displayed at bargain prices are cooly ignored while unsatisfactory services on bargain deals will be complained about. He will

not compromise his standards in the least bit. Your true Brit as I said before, is a critical chap and demands one thousand percent value for his money. Don't forget that the epitomy of stinge, Mr Ebenezer Scrooge, was a Brit and, boy, did he extract every ounce of Bob Cratchet's services for the bargain salary he paid.

It matter's not if they are from the upper classes or the hoi polloi; your true Brit must get his bargain one way or the other. Even their weather has learnt to co-operate by offering them a bargain summer season once a year! So far, the only sector that has staunchly resisted caving in to this bargain demand are the black cabs. It is yet unheard of for a black cab to offer bargain fares. Still one never knows, the miracle may yet happen one of these days.

So, if in the past week you have not surfed the web to find a bargain winter get-a-way package nor purchased a "buy one, get one free" item, or cut out a "50p off with this voucher" from a magazine or even purchased a day-saver bus ticket or cheap day return train ticket, then I'm afraid you can not in any way, consider yourself as being bargainly British!

UPPER AND LOWER CASE
- AN OVER VIEW OF CLASS

I am sure that by now, you are already on your way to being British or at least recognizing a true Brit if you are not one yourself. But just in case there are any loose knots left to tie up, this final segment will put the seal on your Brit-pack and send you confidently on your way to being British. Firstly, we shall deal with some general aspects of the true Brit before going to the specific classes that make up the British society.

On a general note, your average Brit is a law-abiding fellow who believes more in dialogue than in violence, except when pushed against the wall. Then you will see the British Bulldog in real action. The law-abiding characteristic of this race has resulted in a benign police-force (with the possible exception of inner city forces, who through circumstances have had to toughen up and roughen up) who carry nothing more threatening than a truncheon and a radio on their regular beat. Rarely will you see heavy display of force or firearms by the local Bobby, whose activities may even include catching truant children and returning them to the safety of their schools.

The British are not prone to large families as a whole, neither do they tend to practice the extended family system where all live and share alike. They are not particularly religious albeit the Church of England was founded and is headed by their monarchy. Most churches are therefore struggling for existence while some have ended up in the hands of estate agents, for residential conversion. Being a practical kind of person, your average Brit adapts to his environment and circumstances. He drives small, fuel-efficient cars for easier manoeuvring on the narrow British roads and for minimization of pollution. He is environmentally aware, likes reading maps and driving himself.

Cooking is a favourite hobby of the British male and female, which partly explains the proliferation of eating outlets of all types in the nation. Good cookery books are usually guaranteed to reach the bestseller list while cookery programmes are avidly watched on television.

So much for being British. At this point it may it necessary to enlighten you about some classes of Brits you are bound to come across in the realm of the Brits. Top of the list of course, is the House of Windsor. This is the British Royal Family, the living embodiment of Britain's glorious past, stable present and hopefully, its future. They go hand in hand with Buckingham Palace. The Royal Family is an enigma. Nobody, except themselves, can claim full expertise on them, regardless of what you might read.

They let you know only what they want you to know. The Queen is rumoured to be fabulously wealthy. They are Britain's greatest tourist attraction. They also provide endless entertainment to a curious and fascinated nation and generally remain a symbol of stability and continuity in a world of rapidly changing trends. They define class and etiquette. They love their pets and horses and value their privacy as much as press invasions would permit. In conclusion, the Royal Family are the definitive embodiment of what Being Traditionally British is all about. Emulate them if you can ...and if you dare!

Second on the list of classes are the upper class. These are the aristocrats and priviledged nobles of the realm with ice cold blue blood frosting in their refined veins. For the most part, they reside in old ancestral homes in sprawling grounds that date back hundreds of years with an equal amount of history attached to them. You can usually find them in the countryside although most of them own second and third houses in the more fashionable parts of the cities of London and Edinburgh, to name but a few. At other times, you can catch them at theatres, charity events or in the occasional vintage car on their way no doubt to the exclusive private clubs they belong to. In accent, clothing and habits, they are perfect clones of the Royal Family to whom some of them are even distantly related. They love their pets and their gardens and also enjoy those horsey sports previously mentioned. They may not be particularly loaded - certainly not with the British taxation system - but they never fail to keep up appearances in that subdued and drab elegance that screams nobility and class! They pride themselves in being, or at least, appearing to be totally emotionless and in perfect control of their feelings and environment. They are all inevitably products of exclusive private schools, and Oxford or Cambridge, that is if they do go on to higher education. And of course, in the most part, they are Tories and unlikely to be recipients of social benefits. They are equally unlikely to openly enjoy reading the tabloids except perhaps on the sneak. Need I add that there is a preconception that they do not as a rule swear except to say "bloody" and "goodness gracious!". However, a stint with them soon puts an end to this theory. One may be pleasantly surprised to hear them happily flinging the four-letter words here and there amidst the "what ho" and "jolly good". But in formal gatherings amongst outsiders, it becomes a different matter altogether, as decorum takes precedent. In conclusion, these true blue are as truly British as it is possible to be.

Third on our class ladder are the British middle class, with warm pink blood trickling through their bourgeois veins, though some of them might opt for grey blood - regretfully not quite blue but thankfully, definitely not red. The middle class are supposed to be split-level, between upper and lower. But for the benefit of simplicity, we shall keep them one, namely, the bourgeoisie. On the whole, they are the landed and loaded gentry. Equally, mainly products of exclusive public schools, they love exotic holidays, gardening, social events and refined fashion. They can be found in the upper echelons of commerce and industry, the judiciary and medical professions and other professional disciplines. Among the middle class also, are the country gentry, bastions of the nation's food and agricultural industries. These country Brits are hardworking, honest and down-to-earth folks, Britishly drab, fiercely independent and quietly loaded. They have no time for high fashion or high living. Theirs is a life of toil as they work and fight with the elements, EU and national policies, pestilence and the variances of nature. These country Brits are the true McCoy of Her Majesty's realm.

Fourthly, we have the working class, the hoi polloi, with red hot, normal, human blood coursing through their common veins, amply diluted by pints and gallons of lager consumed on a daily basis at the local pubs. They can usually be found in their mortgaged houses, council houses, rented houses or even on the open streets as vagrants. These are the masses, the salt, pepper and onions that spice up the realm. Bold, proud, witty, chauvinistic, taciturn, suspicious and fiercely patriotic, they epitomize the simplest and yet the most complex of all the classes of the British realm. Your working class man can be alternatively humorous and dour, friendly and aloof, depending on his mood. He generally handles responsibility well, otherwise, you may well be looking at the world's greatest loafer cum dosser, whose permanent abode would be the Benefits Office, the bookmakers and the local pubs. On the whole however, the working class man is easy-going. He speaks his mind even if he has to swear liberally to get his message across. He is not averse to resolving issues with his fists should the need arise. He is not particularly concerned about the affairs of the rest of the world except for holiday purposes. He considers himself a D.I.Y expert, loves challenges and shuns the easy way. He is cynical and detests pretentiousness, attempts at social climbing and superficial behaviour of any kind. In conclusion, your working class person (with the exceptions of perverts, psychos and prejudiced prats that equally abound in other classes,) is generally a pretty decent chap and is without doubt, a true Brit.

And finally, the last on our British class menu are the townies. These are the city Brits, the proud guardians of contemporary and cosmopolitan Britain. They are the supporters of all that is flash, brash, loud and new. They are fast, hot, brusque and at times, rude. To them belong the night- clubbing scene, the red-light areas and the literary or arty haunts. Among the townies, you will find the weird, individualistic and flashy fashion trends, ranging from punk to haute-couture, gothic to ascetic, dreadlocks to skinheads and fashion victims of all kinds. The townies have a myriad of accents that broadly reflect the influences of the various races living in close proximity with them as tourists or students. Be it Rap, Rave, Rock or Reggae, straight, Gay, Bi or Freaks, the townies will give you ample leather and silk, vibrant colours and sounds. They are ambitious, religiously, politically and morally tolerant and can easily pass as citizens of any other cosmopolitan city in the world.

The townies love shopping, eating out and experimenting with fashion. They are addicted to their mobile phones and the web and more likely to be interested in the stock exchange than in the affairs of Westminster. They are a mixed breed of, Tories, Labour, Lib-Dems and all other independent parties going. You will find Brits of all colours and creed among the townies. In essence, these city Brits are the Brits that have embraced the spirit of change and done away with the attributes that typify the true Brit while still essentially remaining valid British citizens.

And with this, I shall bid you adieu!

This has **NOT** been brought to you "by appointment to Her Majesty, the Queen".

Alex Stranger-Onoh